SOME PEOPLE /

Jackson Phoenix Nash (he/him) is a queer transgender writer and teacher from Essex. His poetry and fiction have appeared in *Propel*, *Under the Radar*, *Rattle*, *Channel*, *Baffling Magazine* and many more. Jackson is a fellow of the Lambda Literary Writer's Retreat for Emerging LGBTQ Voices. He was shortlisted for the Creative Future Writer's Award in 2020, and in 2022 was selected for Creative Future's Next Up development programme. His PhD in Gender Studies explored trans YA fiction and popular culture.

First published in 2024 by Little Betty, an imprint of Bad Betty Press
Cobden Place, Cobden Chambers, Nottingham NG1 2ED

badbettypress.com

PB ISBN: 978-1-913268-70-1
EPUB ISBN: 978-1-913268-71-8

A CIP record of this book is available from the British Library.

Book design by Amy Acre

Supported using public funding by
ARTS COUNCIL
ENGLAND

LOTTERY FUNDED

Some People Are Trains

JACKSON PHOENIX NASH

For Alice

Whenever I lose my way
you find me
and I am home.

LITTLE BETTY

CONTENTS

BRACES

1.

At school they said I was
too sullen, a teacher took me
into her office and
told me she went through
a phase once and grew

out of it. At school
I grew
increasingly
out of it.

2.

When a seagull goes into shock,
they put a cardboard box
over it to keep it
calm
until the RSPB arrive.

I was under a box
in 6th form, made of a Slipknot
t-shirt and Prozac.
I made myself
a target
that teacher said. She said
I was putting myself
in a box.

3.

'We can't actually talk
about that
kind of *thing* anyway.'
(And she couldn't even add
in a whisper

                                   '*Because of*
           section 28').

Instead,
she said
it was time to go. Put on
a smile. Use
lipstick.

4.

I always had a sore mouth
when I smiled, from years
of braces
tearing the inside
of my cheeks. Shutting
my mouth hurt

as much
as opening it.

CRADLING A DISASTER 30 FEET
IN THE AIR

'It's unclear why the train didn't stop.'
– Reese Oxner, *NPR*, 2nd November 2020

When I was a kid they tried to straighten my teeth with
    train tracks.
Rogue wires and lacerated cheeks, that stretching
    soreness,
pain and interdental brushes chugging daily through the
    tunnels
between cemented brackets
to sculpt my smile

into something more acceptable.

Maarten Struijs sculpted two plastic whale tails
for Spijkenisse station, completely unaware
that 20 years later they'd save a train driver's life,
carriages caught by a fishy appendage
cradling a disaster 30 feet in the air –

I wore a t-shirt once when I was feeling brave that said
'Some people are trans, get over it' and people kept
misreading it as 'Some people are trains.'
And at the time I thought they were wrong,

but now I wonder.

Mermaids are often used as a metaphor
for trans bodies
and I dream for a minute that these
aren't whale tails at all
but the lower halves of trans people,
hiding top surgery scars
below concrete, hiding
from the orthodontist,
pliers poised to snip
train tracks.

I'm lacerated
by fears that puncture my cheeks,
        threaten to show
my trans teeth, still crooked
in the classroom I'm working in now
on a Thursday

where young men talk every week about the grossness
    of queers,
and the things they'd like to do to women, and I shrink
to become one of a million indistinguishable plankton
swimming towards the maw of a whale

                until I hear across the water

that workers are making a sling
                to lift a Dutch train
from a whale tail
to safety.

MEN'S TOILET HAIKU

Flushing, wait for them
to leave, boys who might see through
your clothes, your beard, you.

PINK HANDFISH

'As per their name, the species has over-sized "hands"
on which they "walk" along the seabed in addition
to swimming.' – *BBC News*, 24th December 2021

They thought it was nearly extinct,
unseen since 1999,
the year my Spice Girls posters came down,
who 'as per their name[s]'
had distinct personalities.

I used to be able to 'walk'
on my 'hands' for a second or two,
in the years before the Spice Girls posters
came down, somewhere in Essex.

I'd lean and fall, 'swim' to Earth.
The imprints of garden stones on my palms refilling,
fresh blood singing
the stupid harmonies of youth, gone soon.

This was when I was still a startled '[girl]'
and weighed only 1 gram
more than the air on which I floated
'in addition to swimming'
through the horror of 'walk[ing] along'
as a '[girl]'.

CALL ME BOY ON SATURDAYS

We knocked doors
and when a yes came for a carwash
we asked if they'd fill our bucket,
removing the sponges and chamois,
the bottle of car shampoo
from the local garage
and hand over that green plastic money-maker
to quench our thirst for coins.

We scrubbed, suds
rippled in rivulets
swallowed
by thirsty gaps in the bonnet,
and if they didn't have a hose
(*oh God, please have a hose*),
we'd ask for another bucket load,
two, three, four, to rinse our labour
from car to drain to pocket,
endless heaving, hurling,
watching water
                    hang

for slowly curling moments in the air
before exploding
over clean windshields
and us.

Two kids, 10 years old,
we sold our wiper blade arms,
our skinny *please sir* charms,

bargaining hard
with Michael's Dickensian urchin smile,
fuelled by that never-ending gasoline of *Saturday!*,
giving sponge baths
to the red rust-buckets of Galleywood,
pail hanging jaunty in the crook of my best friend's arm.

At his mum's council flat
we'd count the pennies,
he'd claim extra for the sponges
or the shampoo, the chamois,
anything he thought I'd forget to tally,
but I never argued,
let it spill easy from my mind
like the cheap cola we poured on the pavement
just to watch it fizz.

Because I was there
for the old man downstairs with failing eyes
who thought we were cousins,
the outlines of our matching blonde curtains
and black t-shirts – mine Taz, his Sonic –
washing rheumy into something related.
He'd shuffle out into the bleach-stinking stairwell,
stalling, searching for something
to wipe away the boredom, anything
to drive some conversation.
In his hand a bag, shaking
hard sticky sweets we'd never eat,

and then he'd ask my favourite question:
How many cars did you wash today, boys?
and I silently prayed for Michael
not to ever laugh,
not to ever, ever say what I was,

or what I wasn't.

PORTRAIT OF THE ARTIST
AS A GEEZERBIRD

I was known by the local kids
as Geezerbird, an Essex term
for tomboy, ladette, ugly,
he-she.
I pulled the heads off Barbies,
dressed the torsos up
in GI Joe's fatigues.
Him and Barbie
were both smooth down there
like me.
I pretended to give a shit
about football stickers, Transformers and fighting
and while we all still had high-pitched voices
I could blend.
Geezerchameleon.

Later on, my first said
You fuck like a boy.
Not so much a compliment
as a statement. I covered my teen girl
scent in Lynx
to stink like a boy.
Anything not to become
the delicate bird
they wanted me to.
I pulled the feathers out,
one-by-one, dressed myself
in combats like GI Joe.
Real smooth.

MY LINE MANAGER HELD HER
FATHER'S UGLY TOMATOES

up to the camera, mutated,
bulbous, others withered
like the small, bored faces in boxes
at 4pm in this Zoom meeting,
suddenly so earthy.
Basil-scented over the faint
smell of burning, overheated plugs
hot enough to slow cook
ourselves on.

They spin
slowly on the vine
as she dangles them so close to the camera
that her eyes become succulent
red orbs, frozen
at the ripest moment,
pending connection.

I chose the plain wall as my background:
nothing grows, just oily ghosts
of Blu-tack. It's not the opposite wall
with the Claude Cahun photo
and the painting of women
in a circular march, ouroboros
of breasts, plum, cherry,
on the door

of my cupboard full of men
's clothing.

Someone thrusts
a juicy compliment at those most natural,
blemished balls
of goodness,
that when cooked will break out
of their skins, pink flesh
pulpy, the way it must have looked
before they sewed me back up
after they cut
my boobs off.

My turn
to introduce myself, say
my name,
declare my pronouns,
wait
to wither or ripen,

            to spin
          slowly on the vine.

CLAUDIA

The visiting nightjar flies away, vampiric acceleration,
            splitting   the laptop screen
into MS Teams
                                and an osprey nest,
live-streaming a single bird,
feathers nearly stripped off by the wind.

While I work from home
her absent mate is unreachable on Zoom,
he's off surfing   distant currents
without a username
while she waits, watching her blue screen
of Poole harbour and the forever sea.

On other remote worker's screens
there's porn,
an Easter egg of the Covid-19 crisis –
typing one-handed –
but I'm with the 277 users watching live,
ghosting the chatroom,
this bird known only to them by the code
clipped to her leg, but I can't help
naming her,

my Claudia.
You can rewind her
up to 14 hours, and while it's my daylight
through a red light filter I watch her 2am,
see her friend, the tawny owl's demonic   twisting head
a green ghost in night vision.

The feathers of boredom, the infertile promise
that we are all making the best of it.
When the call finally ends
my colleague's face distorts demonic,
twisting like Claudia's body when she forced
out the first osprey egg laid in England for 200 years,
unfertilised without her mate.

That's what happens
when you do something extraordinary –
277 people you didn't want to show up
do.

She buries her egg,
now rotting as fast as the cursor clicks.

277 people speed her up
until it disappears.

THE SEA EAGLE

dives to eat carrion, stale
fried chicken in a cardboard coffin
at the M40 Welcome Break.
He spells his real name
in the remains in the car park,
not G393,
a juvenile delinquent raised
by conservationists
on the Isle of Wight.

                    I write Phoenix with my bones
                         in the ashes, not _____,
                    still a juvenile delinquent
                    settling into this trans body,
                    with its growth, its new hair,
                 raised by myself. No conservation.

Now he's out on licence
with a VHF transmitter,
colour-ringed, striking, cutting
sharp green lines on a GPS map –

                         I watch him transition
                    from captive to monitored.

But some things
are best seen
from the sky.

Like his tibia flourishes
for detail, his signature
brushstroke in the dirt
at the funeral of a black-backed gull
in the North York Moors,
the decomposing
sculpture of field mice in Norfolk,

                        – my decomposing girlhood –

the bank vole entrail portrait
laid out for visitors
by the River Sheaf
in Sheffield.

                        And while I paced
                        restless in isolation
                                on lockdown,
                grounded by dysphoric meltdowns

he was tagging his way
in bones
through England's towns.

He drops vertebrate marrow
like paper masks, like trucker's
pasty wrappers
in Oxford, off the M40.
His palette isn't limited
by the synthetic nature
of paint. His is the yellow
of calcification,

                              mine the blue, pink, and
                              white, the fresh human
                              red as the pride badges
                              cut
                              into my chest,

a refinement
of blood, in madder,
in crimson, viscera
shining in moonlight, death's blue-treacle,

occasional shreds of missed
flesh and gristle,

 the scars under my nipples that still haven't fully healed

that connective tissue
drawing him   /drawing me
into the land.

MYCENA INCLINATA

a perfect chiaroscuro
on a winter lunchbreak
fawn cap shooting
through a split
in the damp-blackened stump
frilly stipe a filament the width
of 20 human hairs
absorbing life
through mycelia
frilly petticoat catching
the nearlynothing breeze

MUDLARKING

The tide is a smashed up charity shop,
delivering to your feet broken plates and a Victorian fork
to eat the mystery of roof tiles, breezy silver tankards,
doll heads and unclassified innards.
There are risks:
needle stick injuries,
  death by drowning,
    infection,
      premature   elation
when you think you've found an extraordinary relic
but it's only a red balloon
from a 70s stag do.

52 used condoms washed up just this morning
and under your wellies an important clue in a murder case
leaks through
the split in your sole.
You need a permit
and must sift only with your eyes –
in a Wetherspoons pub a friend reveals all this to you,
a new word surfacing in the freshwater foam of a cool
 draft: Mudlarking.

The Thames is so famous it's on the opening credits
of *EastEnders*, the UK's best TV show,
and you know what you want to find:

the arm band of a Viking warrior woman and
   skull fragments,
power-bone particles to craft brew
your own bones in,

because you need to be a warrior right now,
especially in Wetherspoons where you're slightly scared
to take a piss
and for comfort you search 'Mudlarking' on your phone,
as you squat in the cubicle with one foot
pressed hard against the door

                  in case someone should come in
                  and realise what you are.

While they were closed for lockdown
all the best graffiti was alcohol-washed away
so that only the dark blue paint-masked scars of mobile
   sex lines
and football team hate speech
remain –

and now somewhere in the distant dark you hear the
   theme tune of *EastEnders*,
imagine dancing in the water with the doll heads,
caressing your warrior woman's skull,
and hope the lads from the stag do
at the urinals
sift you
only with their eyes.

METRONOME

I stretch out the dawn,
molto rubato, waking
an hour earlier than I need to
from the usual nightmare of bad timing,
crying like a baby. Babies are soothed
by the regular tempo of a heartbeat,
but I'm so used
to the irregular of my own
that I bend time deliberately, try to savour
the slow pulse of pre-rush-hour
cars ticking past on Parkway,
try to make it last
forever. Through glass
it's just the distant sound
of a wire brush on a cymbal,
a rumble, then the delicate
rattle of my windows.

Composed slow coffee, smooth slide
into the Pride flask, measured walk
to the park, to the pond. Family of swans,
necks wound in, gently stirring,
water glistening. They're in the state between sleeping
and waking, neither one thing or the other –
reminds me of my queer piano teacher explaining
glissando, sliding between two notes.
We were always between two notes,
he and I, in the never spoken, in Section 28
– whose magnum opus was that?

A song of silence.

BIGFIN SQUID

Angel hair tentacles,
wispy dancers whipping water,
the longest cat o' nine tails

propelling deep sea particles
with squid arms hinged
as though they have elbows.

Gliding on a genus nickname
– *Magnapinna*, big fins –
it feeds in lazy drags,

lanky grazing, waiting
with noodle limbs,
a passive spaghetti

to receive whatever might pass by
like a depressive's arm
hung nearly pulseless

in a bag of crisps,
occasionally scooping, dipping,
for salty zooplankton, prawn
cocktail.

But this is all speculation,
no one really knows
their feeding patterns,

the sighting last November
in Australia was only number 12.
They fade away

from germs, from crowds,
from the human news
of a nurse, a baby killer, a school closure.

My long fingers, my elbows,
hinging as I turn over,
lazy data-grazing in the squid ink gloom

of the bedroom,
lit only by a news article on a screen. I read
that it lives in the darker parts of the ocean,

that pale ghost of the sea.
I will paint my nails porcelain
in its honour

in the morning, dance
varnished fingers
through the darker parts of the day.

THREADING THE NEEDLE

I mustn't cry in the yoga class.
With each sweep of my right arm
under my body, I am sewing you in

dedicate your practice today to someone you love

All twenty of us begin
to thread the needle
in unison, on all fours. We extend
until the needle points

toward the ceiling
toward the heaven
you believed in

the divine in me sees
the divine in you

We shared the same operation,
double mastectomy.
Mine top surgery,
yours cancer. Sewn up
in the same places
below our hearts,
fourth chakra

inhale
draw your right arm underneath you
rest on the right shoulder

You used to say that when I was excited
I fizzed. You said it again
in the note the solicitor gave me after
you made your decision to

exhale

My chest scars are fizzing now
with this strange stretching
as though ghost stitches
are being tightened

reach the left hand to the sky
open your chest

'life is precious,' you wrote,
'but only as precious
as I say it is'

now take your vinyasa
shoulders back

chest forward

BLUE STARS IN THE MORNING

after Aggregation AP031, Star 7 *by Chun Kwang Young*
(British Museum)

Behind glass, little cardboard boxes
arranged like the cataclysm
of all the world's prescriptions.
At the centre of a star-

burst somewhere inside me, each pill birthed
through a plastic universe
with a foil big bang, ruptures
silver to expand endless

side-effects. You may become sensitive
to sunlight. You may become
sensitive. Attempts to taper off
antidepressants became cosmic

dust in the pill-cutter, nebula
reforming, a false dawn
for broken satellites. Blinking on
and off.

I became sensitive to sunlight.
The sun is a star,
it's just part of a larger phase,
they said, repeating:

one blue tablet a day
in the morning,
at first
light.

I AM DYSLEXIA

After the assessment results
I add a line
to my email signature,
under my pronouns,
above the Trans Staff Network logo.
I want to add *I am dyslexic* in italics
to try to summarise what I actually want to say
which is please
expect two further panicked emails
with my corrections
before you know what I'm trying to ask you.

It comes out
I am Dyslexia.

I am dyslexia,
for 39 years
the spirit guide behind my shoulder
pushing the pen in the right wrong order
that makes me a creative thinker

(apparently).
I thrill at the thought
that I can stop pretending that I understand things
on the first, second, third reading,
that there is a word for I am
just
slower,

there is a word for I have
been faking my way through

forever.
I often write the second letter
of the word first and then go back to give it a face,
or I'll say see when I mean saw
and I've dealt with it before by listening
to my work in Word's monotone read aloud feature
letting waves of mi s ng words and etters sing to me
in a single note.
I am dyslekcia and I wrte everything   in
          fragment s

that have to be   stitched up at the end,
Frankenstein's monster's trans rage
on the page and linear never
but finally something becomes
slowly, it takes so long but finally
something good becomes.

With best wishes

My pronouns are he/him
I am Dyslexia
My normal working hours are hours and hours
and hours   and hours

ACKNOWLEDGEMENTS

Thanks to:

Matt Freidson and Creative Future for the opportunity to be mentored by Caleb Parkin in the *Next Up 2022* writer's development program, and for all the work you do. Caleb's insight, encouragement, and his particular brand of sensitive (yet honest) critiques have been instrumental in the creation of this pamphlet.

All at Little Betty and Bad Betty – Anja Konig for believing in this work and being excited about trains. I can never thank you enough. You are a train. Amy and Jake for all your amazing support.

The editors of *Propel*, *Under the Radar*, *Channel*, *Rattle*, *Impossible Archetype* and *Second Chance Lit* where some of these poems first appeared.

Alice – soulmate, halo-wearing superhero, crazy bird lady, witch, warrior, tiger, and beautiful queer poet with beautiful queer hands. For reading, writing, encouraging, inspiring. I could not have done this without you. Meet me at the bottom of the rabbit hole.

'Call Me Boy on Saturdays' won the *Rattle* Ekphrastic Competition.

Milton Keynes UK
Ingram Content Group UK Ltd.
UKHW012137230524
443117UK00004B/131

9 781913 268701